AF483760

Library of Congress Control Number:
ISBN: 979-8-9947589-9-1



This is a work of non fiction.

This book was printed in the United States of America.
Dedication

# I FELT SAFE WITH YOU

# DEDICATION

This book is dedicated to you. When life stretches you beyond what you think you can handle, remember to extend yourself grace. Challenges may bring failure, shame, or guilt. Those feelings do not get to define you nor are they welcome to stay. Left unattended, they can grow—but when faced with honesty and care, they lose their power, and you begin to heal. Life will make its deposits, some unexpected, heavy, and undeniable, you still get to choose what you carry forward. You will feel deeply, and in those moments, you get to choose growth over retreat. Do not silence your emotions—listen to them. Give yourself permission to feel, to reflect, and to remain present. When clarity feels distant, the mind invents stories born from fear rather than truth. Lay those stories down. Write. Speak. Breathe. Honor every emotion as a messenger, not a sentence. You are not defined by the storm you are in, but by the way you stand within it. This season is not breaking you—it is shaping you. You are becoming, and that is powerful.

# Table of Contents

# Chapter 1

## I Left, you Entered

*You've been the one I've turned to in*
*moments of despair,*
*When God and friends felt far away,*
*and family was not there.*
*I met with you in secrecy,*
*in the shadows masked by night,*
*fearful that my time with you would soon*
*be revealed by light.*
*Courted by the ecstasy experienced within*
*your touch,*
*the warmth and thrill of its release had me*
*thirstily in its clutch. . .*
*and I enjoyed it there.*

When Rayanne first locked in with her addiction, it was a subtle engagement. She was feeling alone. Abandoned. Forgotten. Her pride was left open amidst a pride of hungry vices. Often, we convince ourselves that we could never be weakened to the point of falling prey to a habit or developing a dependency on something external of self. There was an emptiness inside her longing to be filled, to be satisfied. Open spaces rarely remain open for long periods of time. Dressers become a place of storage for jewelry boxes, perfumes, and trinkets. Countertops become overcrowded with coffee makers, mixers, crockpots and utensils holders. If you are not careful or intentional about what you place in the open spaces, it may become cluttered with undesirables.

*An introduction with the undesirable assigned to Rayanne took place in her living room. It found her. It gripped her and it filled her empty spaces.*

The year they met was overwhelmed by changes. She wasn't informed enough to know what was happening in her body nor mind. Reacting to the waves of discomfort rippling throughout, she moved in unsteady, erratic motions. Uncertain of this feeling she had no other option but to surrender and find a way to release.

Rayanne had left the home she had grown to know as "mine. . .all mine." Living in a three story, 4-bedroom row home with her grandmother, in Baltimore, Maryland felt safe. One day, her world was interrupted with a phone call. As her grandmother's face contorted and tightened, she knew change was coming her way. Her grandmother shot a glance in her direction with a glare that bore into her. Confused and scared at the same time had her plastered in the center of the kitchen's archway.

"You're going to go stay with your mother now, I don't have anymore use for you. She wants to claim you."

Speechless. Wondering what had she done for her grandmother to feel so comfortable with sending her away as if the years she kept her was meaningless. No——as if she was meaningless.

"Clean this kitchen before I get back," she demanded.

Her cousins stood silently to the side, their eyes meeting in a moment thick with emotion. The intensity in their gaze spoke more than words could. Rae felt a welling in the center of her throat; her eyes began to water. Hurriedly turning to the cabinets to avoid anyone seeing her, she began to do the dishes. Filling the sink with hot, soapy water, transferring the pain to small, slender hands. They began to redden in the scalding water, and the tears continued to fill up in her eyes. In that moment, their eyes met. Her grandmother looked at her as if she wished she could rewind that entire scene but couldn't; she turns to leave with her grandchildren in toe.

After finishing the dishes, Rae reluctantly called . . .. her mother, Rachael. As the phone rang, she headed upstairs to her bedroom. The realization that this might be the last time she entered her room, pull the blinds, and sink into her bed made the moment unbearably heavy. Pen in hand, she wrote what her heart was crying out.

Desperation gnawed at her as she struggled to understand how her sense of safety could turn into rejection so quickly. How could someone she saw as her refuge so effortlessly let her go. She started packing a few things just as her mother answered.

"Hey Rayanne."

"Hi Mom. Can you come get me?"

"Yes," she answered with curiosity in her voice.

Her mother made her way to her hometown, no questions asked. As Rachael pulled up, her grandmother arrived too, her presence tightening something in Rae's chest. On the dining room table laid the pain-stricken letter addressed to "Mom." Inside were the words that broke Rae's heart and the key to the house. Rae and her grandmother passed one another in the narrow hallway to the front entrance. In her eyes, she found the words she had been waiting for—words she couldn't bring herself to say.

Once they were in the car, she felt her mother's gaze burn into her, though she said nothing. Reclining as they drove on, the crowded row homes fell behind them, replaced by sprawling trees and single-family homes surrounded by full yards. She wasn't in Kansas anymore.

"I'm not going to force you to talk. You can get unpacked and rest. We can talk in the morning if you want to."

As she leaves the room, a call comes. It was Rae's aunt. The family must be well aware of what took place tonight. Her mother circles back to her room and says, "Your aunt wants to speak with you," and hands her the phone. "Hi Rae. You don't have to talk baby, just listen." She begins to pour into her and speak to the pain that she was feeling. She recounted a painful chapter from her youth and how she overcame it, hoping her story would bring Rae some measure of comfort. Rae listened, but the question of how she knew what had happened that evening pressed hard against her thoughts. The phone rang continuously. Once the truth of the evening spread through her cousins, her mother's sisters called, each ring was another reminder of what had unraveled.

Finally, the calls ceased. Sleep had called her, and she was cradled in its arms.

Back at the house, her grandmother opens the letter:

*Mom, I don't understand what I did to make you stop loving me. Tonight, I was made to feel as though I only mattered if you were receiving a check for me. I will always love you and be grateful that you took me in and cared for me. I am sorry if I have become a burden. My heart is broken. You have been my mother and my best friend, and today it feels like that was taken from me.*

*I love you.*

*Rayanne*

Tears filled her eyes as anger rose within her, and she tore the letter into several pieces. She retired to her room, weighed down by the day's events.

Once the morning came, Rae's mother agreed to take her to gather the rest of her belongings. This was now her reality. She was living with her mother in a town called Towson, Maryland. The neighbors were of a certain age and there weren't many children in the neighborhood. Long walks and trips to the corner store became her routine before school resumed.

She had transferred out of district after moving in with her mother. Starting a new school, desperately trying to "fit in" but, unsuccessful on every bend. The hallway glances and stares were taken personally as if they knew her and could see into her insecurities. Retreating into stairwells away from crowds and whispers, she found a moment to herself.

"Rayanne? Rayanne Whitaker?" inquires Mrs. Carson. She was the English teacher. Standing at 5'11 with shoulder length, burgundy colored hair, and dark brown eyes. She appeared to glow as the light breaking through the large rectangular shaped windows framed her. This image crystalized in her memory and was of great significance for how she would come to view Mrs. Carson as the angel in her life.

Mrs. Carson's presence created a disruption in her negative self-talk session on the stairway, breaking up the internal fight Rae was having.

"Yes. I am a new transfer."

"I know. You're in my 5th period class. How are you adjusting?"

"I'm. . .I'm.."

Quickly recognizing that she was at a loss for words, Mrs. Carson shields her uneasiness with a calming tone.

"It will get easier. If you need anything I am here. I'll see you later today," she says with a gentle smile.

In that moment Rae was unaware Mrs. Carson would become an important figure in her high school education and life.

Mustering up just enough desire to make her way to class, fighting through hoards of athletes and cheerleaders taking up space because. . .they could! She begins her trudge down the long hallway. Bumped by clusters of teens identifying as goth, geeks, mean girls, and misfits, she lost her footing. Brrrrring! The bell rings for the 5th period class. Walking into a classroom filled with faces and wage brackets alien to herself was a culture shock. Her eyes scan the room catching the passing of notes under desks. In the corner was a spiky blonde haired football player sucking his finger and sticking it in the ear of the boy seated in front of him. Across the room is the girl who is about to fall to the floor because her classmate thinks it's funny to pull her chair out just as she is about to be seated. There was an empty seat positioned directly in front of Mrs. Carson's desk next to Mei Xin. Her eyes followed Rae all the way to her seat. She leans in and says, "Are you Rayanne?"

"Yes."

"I'm Mei Xin or "Mei-Mei." I couldn't wait to meet you. You're in my Latin class as well.

Everyday Mr. Coup would loudly announce your name 'Raaaaayaaaane!!!'" forgetting we were in class her voice escalates and reaches the height of the room.

"Mei Xin," Mrs. Carson warns with the simple mention of her name and raise of her brow.

"My apologies Mrs. Carson," Mei Xin replies.

"Nice to meet you Mei-Mei," I whisper.

She smiles and turns to the lesson. The classroom was creatively decorated with mannequins styled in attire from The Great Gatsby. That era came alive in a small square shaped classroom laced with beads, feathers, and flapper dresses. That day she fell in love with the roaring 20's.

On that same day, the fragile sense of safety she carried after leaving her home in Baltimore, Md. was completely torn away.

Rayanne never recognized that the attention on her was dangerous. The one watching, saw her and placed claim without contest. He chose entitlement over consent. His smile hid what his thoughts were conjuring in the darkness of his mind. The offense was hauntingly familiar, yet different. She tried to disappear from the vileness of it, her voice was swallowed, just as the act was. The person she turned to for salvation turned from her in what felt like dismissiveness.

"I'm scared. I don't feel safe anymore."

"I'll take care of it Rae. I promise it won't happen again."

"How can you promise that!? I don't feel safe."

"I SAID I WOULD TAKE CARE OF IT!" her mother yells and leaves the house as she headed to work.

The shield of protection that she had come to trust was shattered. Knowing that her mother's promise would be broken, Rae retreated within herself. The house was empty, and Rae was left alone with her fears and herself. Sitting in the living room, wanting to disappear while visions plagued her. Faces, hands, touching her, tearing away at her innocence. The visions poured in like an angry flood. She was determined to make it stop! The tip of her nail began carving trails across her inner arm. It created a vortex for the whirlwind of emotions circling within. Struggling to focus, while inside her, chaos spun wildly —unseen, unnoticed, relentless. Her own voice was still. Everything was now calm.

Rayanne is not unlike many who face pain so heavy that silence feels like the only safe place to hide. Her choices, though difficult, were born from confusion, fear, and a deep need to make the pain quiet. When we look at her journey, we are not asked to judge but to understand. To see how loneliness, loss, and unspoken hurt can grow into something we don't recognize until it's already taken root inside us.

As you take a moment to reflect, think about the spaces within yourself, the ones that feel empty, confused, or unsettled.

Healing begins when we name what lives there and choose what to fill those spaces with.

Let's explore those spaces together in the next activity.

*This is an invitation to notice, not to judge. The emotions that appear on your map are not problems to fix—they are signals asking to be seen.*

*You do not need to name everything at once, and you are not required to go deeper than feels safe today. Some emotions may feel clear; others may feel tangled, distant, or heavy. All of that is allowed here.*

*If something stirs discomfort or overwhelm, pause. Breathe. Step away if needed. You are in control of this process. Reflection is not about reliving pain—it is about increasing awareness with compassion.*

*There is no "wrong" emotional landscape. What you feel makes sense in the context of what you've lived. And like Rayanne, simply noticing your inner world is already an act of courage.*

*Move slowly. Be kind to yourself. This is the beginning of learning how to listen to what your heart and mind have been carrying.*

**Reflective Activity: "Mapping My Emotional Landscape" Chapter 1**

Objective

To help readers identify and process their emotions safely.

To explore triggers, coping strategies, and self-care tools.

To connect personally with themes from Rayanne's story (depression, emotional overwhelm, self-awareness).

Materials Needed Notebook or journal

Pens, colored pencils, or markers Optional: stickers or highlighters

Step 1: Create Your Emotional Map

Draw a large circle in the center of the page and label it "Me Today."

Around the circle, write or draw all the emotions you've been feeling recently, both big and small. Examples: sadness, anger, loneliness, hope, love, fear.

Use colors to reflect intensity: darker or brighter colors for stronger emotions, lighter for subtler ones.

Step 2: Identify Triggers

Next to each emotion, write what you notice tends to trigger it.

Example: "Sadness → late nights alone," or

"Frustration → too many responsibilities."

Remember, triggers don't define you—they help you understand patterns.

Step 3: Safe Coping Strategies

For each difficult emotion, write down healthy ways to cope.

Examples: journaling, talking to a friend, deep breathing, going for a walk, reading scripture, listening to music.

Include at least one strategy you can try today.

Step 4: Reflection Questions

Which emotion do I feel most strongly right now?

What part of this map surprised me?

When I feel overwhelmed, what is one safe and compassionate step I can take?

How can I treat myself with the same care that Rayanne eventually learns to offer herself?

Step 5: Closing

Take three deep breaths, slowly in and out.

Optional: write a self-compassion statement at the bottom, e.g.,

"It's okay to feel this way. I am doing my best, and that is enough."

"I am allowed to take small steps toward healing."

Facilitator Notes (if used in a group)

Emphasize confidentiality and safety—this activity is reflective, not a disclosure requirement.

Encourage participants to pause if any part

feels triggering and use grounding techniques. Reinforce that help is always available if emotions become overwhelming (provide hotlines or local resources).

# Chapter 2 Healing in Motion

Fragmented pieces fixed together in order to be showcased before the world, not to heal but to be shown.

Performing for an audience unaware they were watching an act. Rayanne learned to masquerade behind masks in hopes to hide from an ugliness she believed she escaped long ago. Her appearance had changed drastically as she began to restrict her intake, her frame became thin and gaunt.

Who was this once vibrant, full of life teenager dressed in oversized clothing and paled complexion? Her presence was swallowed by the crowds filling the hallways and spilling out of the overpacked cafeteria. Mrs. Carson found her sitting alone, away from the overcrowded areas.

"Rayanne, you are welcomed to sit in my classroom if you'd like. . whenever you'd like."

Looking into Mrs. Carson's face, staring intently into her eyes wanting to be transparent in that moment but did not.

"Thank you," she replies with a smile.

Standing to her feet she loses her balance and faints. Rayanne regained consciousness in the nurse's station after her mother was called and told she was being sent to the hospital. When her mother arrived, Rayanne was in a room connected to an IV drip and resting. Rachael went to the nurse's station to get updates on her daughter.

"Hello. I'm Rayanne's mother. Can I talk with someone about her care?"

"Yes. I'm her nurse. Shirley. Mom, what is your name?"

"Rachael Whitaker."

"Thank you, Ms. Whitaker. Let's go into the room."

Rachael follows the nurse into an empty visiting room near Rayanne.

"Your daughter was brought in after fainting. The school informed us that this was not the first incident. Rayanne is severely dehydrated. Testing indicated decreased serum T3 levels, along with multiple deficiencies—primarily iron, zinc and vitamin D, followed by copper, selenium, and vitamin B1. She has been diagnosed with anorexia nervosa."

"What does this all mean?"

"We will keep her on the IV drip and get her levels stable. We have social work paged to come and speak with you. Outside services may be helpful in addressing your daughter's eating disorder."

"Thank you, Shirley. Thank you!"

"Do you have any questions about what we discussed?"

"No. I just want to see my daughter." "Of course."

Entering her daughter's hospital room weighed heavily on her heart. Her eyes scanned her child's profile, then the stillness—the blankets scarcely marking that a body was there at all. She was skeletal in appearance. How had she not known? how had she not felt it, when illness had hollowed her child from the inside out? Rachael pulled up a chair next to her daughter and held her hand.

"Rae."

Eyes barely opening, she looks in her mother's direction."

"Rae, is this my fault? I'm so sorry."

She had no strength to answer, no energy to carry her mother's guilt, and so she lay there, utterly motionless beneath its weight.

Following her discharge, Rayanne returned home with her mother. She consented to therapy with a woman she knew from church, believing familiarity might soften the walls. Ms. Monica served as an evangelist at the church and maintained a private practice of her own. Rachel believed this would be a good fit, given her daughter's quiet resistance to opening herself to strangers.

After two weeks, Rayanne's color returned, and with it, a fragile willingness to eat. One day, the therapist deviated from her usual method and ventured into a less palatable subject.

"Rayanne, tell me about your uncle."

Rayanne's expression soured and her voice went silent. The therapist did not force a reply, leaving the words to hang in the air, unclaimed. She waited, saying nothing, letting the stillness do its work.

"In the beginning, I was treated as his own. We all went to work events and outings together. He was fun—attentive, playful. I remember riding on his back through the living room, my hands tangled in his thick afro, laughing without knowing why it felt safe."

"Did something change?" "Yes."

"What changed?"

Rayanne walked toward the door with the hanging mirror, images clawing at her mind which she struggled to keep buried, her composure thinning with every step.

"He changed. The way he saw me. The way he touched me."

She bit her lip, damming the emotions swelling inside her, barely contained.

"My aunt said that he would tell her he had to check on me in the middle of the night."

"Rayanne. Do you want to talk about what would happen in the middle of the night?"

Looking into Monica's direction, Rae continues.

"I remember his hands. His hands on parts of my body that no one was supposed to touch. I couldn't stop him. His hands were so big. So strong. I can still feel them wrapped around my wrist."

"Rayanne, what else do you remember? "I

remember my aunt going into the hospital. It seemed as if she was gone for a stretch of time. My uncle would take my cousins and me into the bedroom and have us remove our clothes. Then we would lay on the bed. His hands were so large, they smothered my body. I can see his eyes staring directly at me. His face moving closer until his mouth reached my inner thighs. It was cold and wet. Then it was over."

"When it was over, where was Rayanne?"

"What do you mean"

"Do you remember being present? Or do you feel as though something allowed you to leave that space?"

"I was present. I remember we would get up and get dressed and go play."

"Was each time different?"

"There were times it was different, yes. There were times he used his hands. There were times he used both hands and his mouth. There were times he had us do the same."

"Do the same? "Yes. To him."

"There is one day that stands out the most for me. We were all sitting in the living room. My oldest cousin was holding us and crying. She kept saying, 'I am going to protect you!' My uncle had other men in the home. I believe that day would have changed our lives completely. My oldest cousin begged for my uncle to take her in place of us—and he did. Each of those men went into the room with her."

Rayanne closed her eyes and the memory of her cousin's rape continued. Her heart broke and the tears came. Ms. Monica refrained from interrupting, recognizing that it might cause her to contain or suppress emotional expression.

"Years later, I had the opportunity to thank my cousin for saving me from that pain. It felt crazy thanking her knowing how it changed her life. She cried and told me she would do it again. That time changed her. It stole from her."

"How did it change you?"

"It gave me another reason to distrust people."

"How did you see Rayanne after that happened?"

"I didn't like myself." "Why?"

"I believed that I was the reason my cousins no longer had their father. If I never went to live with them, that never would have happened."

"Do you believe that today?" "No."

"Rayanne. Thank you for sharing with me.

I know that was challenging. How are you feeling in this moment?"

"Heavy but ok."

"Is there anything else we need to discuss before we close?"

"No"

"Okay Rae. I will see you next week." "Yes." Rayanne's condition was continually improving, and she returned to school wearing wires and medical apparatuses. The physicians expressed concern regarding the frequency of her syncopal episodes and initiated cardiac monitoring. She was no longer seen as a peer, but as something fragile everyone feared damaging. Against medical advice, she removed the device and placed it in her backpack. Instantly, she became "normal" again. Normal. During one of her therapy sessions, she entered with an apple pie. Ms. Monica was silent yet observant waiting for Rayanne to finish eating. As she was about to discard the carton, Monica stood, smiling, and stretched out her hand.

"May I?"

Baffled but curious, Rayanne hands Monica the carton. She walks over to the chalkboard hanging on her wall and removes a tack placing the empty carton on the wall.

"This day. . . you overcame. Let this be a reminder to you!"

Rayanne smiled. The year ended with Rayanne feeling stronger, steadier, almost whole.

In the next activity, we'll explore what it means to rebuild from brokenness to fill the empty spaces not with shame or silence, but with intention, courage, and care.

*Healing is rarely linear, and reflection does not require certainty—only willingness.*

*You may discover that the "small steps" matter more than the dramatic moments. Rest counts. Pausing counts. Noticing what helped, even briefly, counts. If at any point this activity feels heavy, you are allowed to stop, take a breath, or return to it another day.*

**Reflective Activity: "Healing Steps: Mapping My Journey" Chapter 2**

Objective

To reflect on the emotional, physical, and mental challenges Rayanne faced.

To help readers identify personal coping strategies and sources of support.

To connect the concept of healing in motion to their own lives.

Materials

Notebook or journal

Pens, colored pencils, or markers Optional: sticky notes

Step 1: Identify Emotional Moments

Reread the chapter and note three moments where Rayanne experienced strong emotions (fear, sadness, relief, or hope).

Write each moment in your journal or on sticky notes.

Next to each, jot down what helped her cope or begin to heal (e.g., therapy, support from her mother, small steps like eating the apple pie).

Step 2: Map Your Own Healing

Draw a timeline or path across the page.

On this timeline, mark moments in your life where you faced challenges or "heaviness" similar to Rayanne's experiences.

Next to each, write what helped you feel safer, calmer, or supported.

Examples: talking to someone you trust, journaling, taking a walk, prayer, creative expression.

Step 3: Reflection Questions

Which moments in Rayanne's story felt most powerful or relatable to me?

What small steps did she take toward healing

that I can learn from?

How did support from others (mother, therapist) affect her journey?

What does "healing in motion" mean in my own life?

Step 4: Healing Action Plan

Write down one small step you can take this week to care for your emotional or physical health.

Identify one trusted person or resource you can reach out to if you feel overwhelmed.

Optional: Add a symbol, color, or image that represents your personal resilience or progress.

Step 5: Closing Reflection

Take a few deep breaths and reflect on the statement:

"Healing doesn't always happen all at once; it happens in motion, step by step, day by day."

Write a short affirmation inspired by Rayanne's journey:

Examples: "I am capable of small steps toward healing."
"I can reach out for support when I need it."
"I am allowed to feel, to pause, and to grow."

# Chapter 3 Home Sweet Home

High school was a distant memory yet, its ghost still made the hairs on Rae's body stand at attention.

Entering her freshman year at the University of Alabama was meant to be an exciting time, though it would not last long. Exploring neighboring towns and immersing herself in Southern cuisine proved to be an interesting experience.

Classes and social spaces conformed to her with tailored precision, leaving no room for doubt. Rae's introduction to her three roommates was positive and immediately put her at ease. Out of the three there was one of whom would soon become a source of constant torment, Bethany.

During Freshman Introduction, Rae's name was called, instructing her to report to the Bursar's Office. There was an issue with her financial aid. Upon her arrival she met with Ms. Aguilar.

"Rayanne Whitaker!" "Yes. I'm here."

"Let's go to my office. How are you adjusting so far?"

"I am enjoying the town and the people. Thank you for asking."

"That's wonderful! You may have a seat."

"Thank you."

"So, I was looking at your account and there is a remaining balance of $1,200. Would you be able to satisfy this balance in full or shall we break it up in payments?"

"I can pay it today. I can put it on my credit card. Surprisingly, there were different banking groups set up outside and I was approved in a matter of minutes."

"Well, small blessings! I don't think I need to tell someone as intelligent as you my dear but be responsible. I see you have work study. You always want to pay off balances before the billing date."

"I will be able to make payments towards it but, I don't know if I will be able to pay it in full before the billing date."

"Just tuck that information away as something to refer to in the future. I want you to have a successful year and if you have questions or concerns do not hesitate to reach out."

Ms. Aguilar handed Rae a card and thanked her for stopping by.

Within weeks of enrolling and getting acclimated to a new place, Bethany revealed her true self in small, unmistakable ways. Rae noticed the shift before she could name it. Desperately trying to ignore the change in her behavior but failing. Bethany began following her across campus, trifling through her belongings, and watching over her through the night. These behaviors intensified.

After weeks of trying to adjust, illness returned quietly—like a faulty board waiting to snap under weight. Unaware that the damage was already done, she reached out to Ms. Monica, her therapist.

"Hello Ms. Monica." "Hi Rae."

"How are you adjusting."

The line fell silent as Rayanne crumbled under the weight of what she had been carrying alone. Once she was able to put words to the emotional strain she was experiencing, Monica inquired whether a room reassignment was possible. One of Rayanne's roommates had developed an unhealthy infatuation with her. These behaviors caused significant emotional distress and contributed to a sense of fear which triggered past experiences. Rayanne was encouraged to involve the Residential Advisor.

"Rae? I know this is scary for you. But I want you to rely on those that are there to keep you safe. Are you hearing me?"

"Yes. I will speak with the R.A." "Who is there with you Rae?" "A friend."

"May I speak with her?" "Yes."

"What is her name?" "Raushanah."

Monica spoke with Rae's friend to ensure she had someone to be with her as she met with the Advisor. Raushanah was agreeable and informative in regard to the events that had unfolded since Rae had arrived.

Raushanah informed Monica that it was difficult for her to be present most times in order to avoid confrontation. She shared that the roommate was not safe, and she did not feel comfortable with Rae remaining in that room.

Following the report, Rae waited to be moved. Days passed. Her appetite faded alongside her diminishing hope for help. She went to class emptied of motivation, unable to focus, each lecture was another reminder of how meaningless showing up had become. Raushanah painfully watched as her friend retreated within herself.

Choosing self-preservation became an act of mercy, she escaped the slow, relentless grief of watching her friend decline in front of her. There was no one to hold her, nowhere to collapse, no place to release the weight and the evil took its hold.

Following classes, Rae returned to the dorm and was met by the RA. "Hi Rae, do you have a moment?"

"Sure."

"There is another unit available for you to move in today if you are still interested."

Rae wanted to feel excitement. Relief. She felt nothing. The destruction was no longer coming it had already begun its work within her.

As Rae unpacked her things, she was greeted by a soul alive with color, joy, and warmth.

"Hi. I'm Jennifer." "I'm Rayanne."

"Hey Rae Rae," she excitedly responded.

Jennifer's light pressed gently against the parts of Rae that had been starved of safety for so long, parts that recognized warmth even as they feared it. Hopeful that this change might pull her from the despair she had sunk into, Rae opened herself to possibility. Upon Jennifer's return to the room, she found Rae convulsing and barely responsive. Gathering her up in the blanket crumpled beneath her, she pulls her down the hall towards the front desk calling for help. Residents are running out in attempt to assist and calling for the Residential Advisor. Watching as people are running past her with faces filled with concern, Rae lay on the ground defenseless. The Residential Advisor, Tara, hovered close, her touch careful as she smoothed Rae's hair and face, her expression heavy with sadness.

The ambulance arrived and carted Rae away. The students were left wondering, sad, hurt, confused.

Rae arrived at the hospital with dangerously low vitals, and clinicians moved quickly—IVs, interventions—to keep her from slipping away. The school had provided the hospital with emergency contact information, and the doctor called Rae's family.

"Good evening, this is Dr. Jamison. I am calling about your daughter Rayanne Whitaker."

"Yes."

"She has been admitted to our hospital in due to decline in vitals. When she presented her body was convulsing and she was not responsive. We have done what is possible at this time, but I am not hopeful.

By the time you arrive, your daughter may

be gone."

Rachel releases a scream and tells the doctor to do everything to keep her daughter alive. She assures him that she would get there to see her child alive. Rachel ends the call and calls Rayanne's grandmother.

"Mom! Mom! Our baby!!"

Her mother immediately secured a flight for her daughter to get to Alabama and bring home their baby.

As the hours pressed on, Rayanne lays in the hospital room interrupted by nurses checking her vitals every hour. She fails to open her eyes until. . . . . she prays within herself. She could not utter words, but she could call to God from within. She prayed, "Father, I am no longer my own."

When the morning came, her mother was

standing over her.

"Rae."

"Mom?"

"Hi Rae. Mommy is here to take you home."

Home? Nowhere felt like home. Rayanne had been disenrolled by the University due to the severity of her illness and condition. She knew she couldn't return to Towson with her mother. Once they got back to Maryland, the family was waiting. Her grandmother was waiting. She stretched out her arms and held Rayanne as though she might never see her again. She invited Rayanne to come back home with her and she accepted.

Rae realized she was not emotionally ready to return to a university at this time. She registered at the community college, part-time enrollment. However, staying busy and having something to occupy her mind felt necessary.

Rae applied for a position at her mother's workplace and was hired immediately. She was offered 3rd shift and was working with a man who presented as honorable, kind, and safe. His name was David.

The nights included deep cleaning, toileting of patients if necessary and monitoring every hour. In between time the two would converse and become familiar with one another's family and life events.

Rae did not sense danger. Following a shift, Rae's car would not start, and David offered to take Rae home. Before reaching her home, he asked if she would be okay stopping at his house. His wife had called, asking him to stop by before taking Rae home—she wanted to meet her.

"Hi. I'm Miriam. It' a pleasure to meet you. My husband speaks of you often."

"It's a pleasure to meet you, Miriam. I am Rayanne." Miriam smiles and stares awhile before looking in her husband's direction as if giving her approval.

"I guess you two should head out."

The meeting was brief and odd. David drives Rae home. That day marked the beginning of a darker turn in their interactions.

The following evening, Rae reported to her shift and the duties had been completed.

"Rae, you can rest," David calls from the back room. "I finished everything before you arrived."

Feeling uneasy, Rae walks through the house scanning over counters, floors, each bathroom, while poking her head into the bedrooms not to disturb the clients. The house was clean. The chores were complete. When she circled back to the front of the house, David was standing in the doorway, blocking her from entering the living room.

"Excuse me."

There was a long pause as he stares into her eyes accompanied by a hauntingly uneasy glare.

"You are so beautiful Rae." "Thank you."

He begins to rub his fingers along her arm. Alarmed she pulls away.

"Don't be scared."

What filled her was fear—pure, consuming, absolute. She becomes frozen.

Still. The rubbing continues. He moves in just as the front door opens. His relief has come.

"Have a good night, ladies," he calls out as if that moment had not occurred.

Relief staff noticed the way David looked at Rae but dismissed it.

"Hey Rae."

"Hey Brandi. Everything has been completed so it should be an easy night."

"Rae are you ok?"

"Yes. . . how was your day?"

"Girl, I have been running all day so coming into an easy night was exactly what I needed."

The evening provided her with that very thing, an easiness. She did not dismiss what she saw; she filed it away, prepared to revisit it if needed.

Weeks went by, and David's behavior crossed further into boldness he no longer tried to hide. Rae's sense of security had been breached, her voice pushed down. His comfort with touching her and invading her space continued to grow. Each night his advances escalated, lacking restraint. Rae arrived at her usual time. Chores were complete.

"Rae!" David angrily calls from the back of the house.

Her senses are warning her not to go in the direction of his voice. The lights are turned off and it would be hours before the relief staff would arrive.

"Rae!"

Ignoring his calls he comes to where she is and asks the question, "Could you hear me?"

"Yes, I could hear you."

Moving in closer, causing her to step back towards the wall with no room for escape, he pins her. Staring into her eyes with a familiar stare. Unbeknownst to her, he had already removed his clothing and left himself exposed. Unable to move, he begins to unfasten Rae's pants and lower her panties. He pressed his mouth to her neck, his grip firm around her wrist. His body is firmly pressed against her and as he is about to enter her, the front door swings open. Brandi came in without warning, driven by an unshakable sense that she was needed. She lunged toward Rae, pulling David away and striking him, fury pouring from her mouth.

He wrestles to pull up his clothes and remove himself from Brandi's grip. As he stands to his feet, she yells. "Get out of here before I call the cops!"

Slithering out of the front door with his head hung low, pulling the door behind him, does not pull Rae from that space.

"Rae! Rae" Calls Brandi.

Her clothes were still hanging from her body, and she was staring off in a distance.

"Rae, he's gone. You're safe. Do you want me to call the police?"

Rae fails to speak.

"You don't have to say anything right now. I'm here with you. No one is going to hurt you."

When Rae's focus turns to Brandi, she falls in her arms. Brandi just held her until she no longer needed to be held.

"Rae, we need to report this to the office." "I can't."

"Then, I will."

When Rae went home the following morning, she couldn't share what happened with her grandmother. She carried the words in silence, unable to let them exist out loud.

"Rae, tell Mommy what's on your mind."

"Nothing. I'm ok."

"You know I see you?"

Rae refuses to speak those events that remain on replay in her mind. Instead, she smiles and assures her grandmother that she was fine.

Rae retreats into the bathroom where she could be alone with her secret thoughts and acts. Pulling a razor blade from her pocket, she raises her left sleeve, and intersecting lines drape her inner arm. Each slit releases the pressure building within her. Rae hadn't seen Monica in months. She knew she was breaking, but stopping her current routine would have meant feeling all of it at once.

*This chapter and reflection may stir memories, sensations, or emotions you did not expect. In the next activity, we will explore the ways trauma can silence the voice and how reclaiming that voice becomes the first act of healing. Nothing that surfaces is wrong, dramatic, or a failure on your part it is simply information asking to be held with care.*

*You are not required to finish this activity in one sitting. You may skip questions, return later, or stop altogether. Reflection is not a test of strength or honesty. It is an act of listening to yourself, to your body, and to what feels possible right now.*

*If at any point the feelings become heavy, pause. Breathe. Look around and remind yourself where you are. Reach for something grounding—a warm drink, fresh air, a trusted voice.*

**Reflective Activity – Chapter 3**

Title: When Home Doesn't Feel Safe

This activity is an invitation, not an obligation. Complete only what feels safe. You may write, draw, sit quietly, or pause at any point.

1.  Grounding Before Reflection

Before beginning, take a moment to arrive.

Place your feet on the floor.

Take three slow breaths.

Name three things you can see, two things you can feel, and one thing you can hear.

When you feel ready, continue.

2.   Finding Yourself in the Chapter

Chapter 3 explores false safety, delayed protection, boundaries being crossed, and survival when the body remembers before the mind can speak.

Reflect quietly or write:

What part of this chapter stayed with you the longest?

Was there a moment where Rae's body knew something before her words did?

Did you notice a time when help came late —or almost didn't come at all?

 Optional writing space:


3.   The Body Remembers

Rae's body responded again and again when

words were unavailable.

Consider:

How does your body tell you when something isn't right?

Where do you feel fear, shutdown, or overwhelm physically?

What signs do you wish someone had noticed sooner?

You may draw an outline of a body and shade or mark areas that respond when you feel unsafe—or simply name them in words.

4.  Redefining "Home"

Throughout the chapter, Rae searches for home—at school, in people, in routine, in work.

Reflect:

What did "home" mean to Rae at this stage of her life?

What does home mean to you?

Is home a place, a person, a feeling—or something else entirely?

Complete one or more of the following prompts:

Home feels like

___________________________________


Home is not

___________________________________


I feel safest when

___________________________________



5.   Silence, Survival, and Shame Rae carries what happened without

speaking it. Not because she is weak—but because she is surviving.

Gently consider:

Why do you think silence felt safer than speaking?

Have you ever held something alone because saying it out loud felt impossible?

What would compassion—not judgment—say to that silence?

💬 Write a sentence to yourself or Rae that begins with:

"You did what you had to do to survive…"

---

6. The Interruptions That Save Us This chapter contains moments where someone steps in—sometimes just in time.

Reflect:

Who intervened when Rae could not protect herself?

What does this say about the importance of witnesses?

Who has ever interrupted harm in your life —big or small? You may list:

A person A moment A decision

A miracle you didn't recognize at the time

7.  Closing Integration

Finish with one of the following:

One boundary I am allowed to have is

_______________________________.

.

# Chapter 4 Trusting The Lie

Deciding that it was time to re-enroll full time, Rae transferred to Morgan State University changing her major to Social Work. Here she met the young man that would change the trajectory of her life. She stuffed her schedule with work, school, volunteering and youth ministry, she would have little to no time for distractions. There he stood, 6'2, midnight hue, with athletic build vying for Rae's attention.

"You're in Statistics class," he says.

"Yes, I am. Can I help you with something?"

"I'm Michael. I was thinking that I could help

you."

"Excuse me."

"I noticed you in session hall in search of a tutor. Math is my strong point. I can help you."

"Oh."

"So, would you like to schedule time to study?"

"I have a very busy schedule. No one was able to accommodate my schedule."

"Well, I have a lot of flexibility. What do you need?"

"I can meet Tuesday or Thursday mornings around 8am or every other Saturdays. My Sundays vary."

"I can meet with you in the morning or on Saturdays."

"Really? Thank you." "You are welcome."

"By the way, my name is Rayanne."

"It's a pleasure to meet you, Rayanne. I will see you Tuesday morning." He hands her a piece of paper with his phone number.

Meeting regularly for the next few months strengthened Rae's trust and allowed her to feel comfortable in Michael's presence. There were no inappropriate gestures or comments. He was a gentlemen and extended patience and care. He was charming. Rae was developing a softness which she could not explain. Michael noticed the change in Rae's glance. It was no longer pained with caution but held a hint of interest. Even still, he remained careful.

"So, I like you," Michael blurts out." Rayanne offered a shy, coy smile.

The two became inseparable. Michael's urges were rising along with his frustrations. Rae was a virgin and expressed her desire to remain a virgin until marriage. Michael had convinced her that there were activities they could partake in which would not compromise her virginity. The closer they got, the more her past surfaced. Rae kept her heavy feelings at bay by cutting. Michael would notice the markings but never dwelled on the topic.

He was the only one she didn't feel the need to hide from either because he didn't care enough or he accepted her. Holding the razor to her flesh, feeling the warmth of her blood created a sense of safety.

Her college years ran like water through her hands, and graduation came and went without pause. Rayanne and Michael's relationship experienced turbulence but was able to withstand. They envisioned the rest of their lives unfolding in bliss.

Wedding plans gave way to bigger dreams of leaving the state and raising a family. Rayanne believed life had traded in its horrifying masks for serenity. What was believed and what was reality conflicted with the other. A dreaded heartbreak waited in the shadows of the lie which their marriage was built. Michael folded under the pressure of his frustrations and fell in the bed, back seat of his Volvo with a female he shared with his best friend. His flesh was too weak to deliver on a promise scheduled for forever. Dreading the unthinkable, he gets the call telling him that he was the father of a baby boy. A truth that would ultimately bring down the structure of Rae's family from within.

Watching as their 2-year-old son runs through the home, laughing, joyfully playing ignorant of what path was now laid before them. Michael said nothing.

Pretending as though the words were never spoken, the message was never received, the call ended. Rae's husband rose from his seat of lies and prepared his mind for that week's meeting at the courthouse——-alone.


Michael turned overtly abusive, leaving his wife exposed to attacks she had neither expected nor understood how to survive.

The behavior towards his wife soured into

open mistreatment, sharp words and cold silences. By withdrawing affection and humiliating her, he caused undeniable harm. Rayanne's physical appearance bore the brunt of her emotional heartache.

Carrying their second child along with the stress of a troubled marriage threatened the pregnancy. Rae's doctor recommended early leave because of the possibility of miscarriage. Even after the discovery of an outside child, Michael's infidelity continued. His propositioning and involvement with other women continued, further eroding the relationship and Rae's mental health. As she had with every other trauma, she buried what she felt and endured the reality in silence.

Rae walked through the next few years in a

deadened state. Wanting to end the relationship while struggling with the thought of failure tugged at her moral compass. Leaving felt necessary; failing felt unforgivable. Yearning for a sense of grounding Rae goes where it feels safe, where she feels home. She goes to see her grandmother.

Sitting outside the 3-story house, staring at the porch remembering days looking up into the heavens, gazing endlessly at the stars, brought calm. Before Rae realized it, her grandmother was standing on the step waiting for her to step out of the car.

"Hi Mom."

"How's Mommy's baby?"

The flat green carpet stretched across the porch beneath her feet. She kept her head lowered, avoiding her grandmother's gaze, eyes capable of unlocking her deepest emotions.

"Rae, you know Mommy knows you?! You can always come home."

"Mom, my heart is so heavy."

"I can feel it. Come on in. Have some tea and something to eat with me."

The two spent the rest of the day completing crossword puzzles and cryptograms, talking through life as the weight Rae carried slowly began to lift.

Gently rubbing the bottom of Rae's chin, her grandmother reassures her, "Baby, you are going to be alright because you are my child! I may not have birthed you, but you are mine!"

Feeling encouraged, Rae stands and readies herself to return home. Whatever home had been, it was gone.

Time moved through Rae quietly, years entered her life and left her changed. She had become what her Aunt Jocelyn feared years ago, "a shrinking violet." Her aunt did not approve of the marriage. Sensing the two were unequally yoked and that knowledge alone was enough for her not give her blessing. Two more children were born of their union before they would experience the final blow.

New Year's Day, Rae was beginning her shift. The day had begun just as every other workday. However, she would not be the same woman at the close of the day. News her husband secretly tucked away 13 years ago, surfaced. Unable to place one foot in front of the next, plastered in the spot where the call came in through her cell phone. On the other side was a faceless woman, her husband bedded imparting pieces of himself creating a life, a child.

"Hello, my name Mya. I know you have probably heard all sorts of distorted versions of who I am, but I don't care. I just want my son to know his family."

"Your son?"

"Yes. My beloved child. His father is your husband."

The call suffocated into silence, trapping Rae inside what had been said.

"Hello. . . . I know you may have your opinions of me and your husband probably ran my name through the mud."

"I have no idea who you are nor has your name ever been mentioned in my household.

I will speak with my husband.”

 When Rae disconnected the call, a weight collapsed inside her, and every second became something to fight through. The receptionist sitting before her noticed a change in her expression.

“Rae? Are you ok.”

Staring blankly, quickly lowering her head she heads back to her office.

Moving and functioning as if her world was not just hurled off its axis. Sitting at her desk, as the calls continued to come through, Rae remained prisoner to the emotion ensued from the words spoken on the call. Sounds stirred from deep within her soul, an aching that could not be soothed. Ms. Johnson, her coworker heard the soft groans, uncertain of the source.

Looking to her left, she witnesses Rae's head and entire frame slump into the wooden encasing encircling the station. Reaching out to her, she raised Rae up and gathered her belongings. No words were spoken; the hush pressed in as they moved toward the exit. Once the air hit Rae's body, the quiet denseness that pressed against her chest released. She collapsed to the ground.

"Rae, you will get up from this place. It will not hold you captive. Do you hear me? You will remember this day and this moment and it will no longer have power over you."

Ms. Johnson walks Rae to her car. Each step was prompted.

"Put the key in the ignition. Breathe. Rae. Breathe."

Rae attempts to take a breath and felt gulps of air clogging her airway.

"Rae. Breathe."

She stayed with her until she was able to move from that space.

"Let me know when you are home. Do not worry I will text Ann letting her know you needed to leave for the day."

The drive from work to home was timeless. Rae could not recall one stop light, building, crosswalk, or billboard along the way. Her commute was on autopilot. She entered the home waiting for her husband to follow close behind. She made one call to him before pulling out of the parking lot at work. "You could have protected me and delivered the news you knew she was calling to give me.

Instead, you let a stranger deliver news that broke my heart.

You could have stopped it, but you didn't."

"Rae. I know. I know."

The call drops after she disconnects on her end.

Rae, did not trust her thoughts nor possible responses and called her cousin who arrived shortly after she walked in the house. Saying nothing, she sits to left of Rae, watching as her stare remains fixed on the entrance of the house. The children arrive first.

"Mom," calls the oldest child Chance.

Her voice flat, lacking emotion, along with the gaze of her stare she replies, "Baby, go to the bus stop and get your sister please."

Upon their return to the house, their father

entered, panting.

"Rae."

Turning to him, blankly, almost mechanic, Rae says, "Tell your children why you will be leaving this home tonight."

Shocked by her words, "I'm not leaving. We need to talk about this."

"Talk to your children," she replies.

Her cousin becoming more nervous with Rae's responses and emptiness in her eyes, she interjects and asks the children, "Do you have anything you need to say to your father or that you need from him?"

"I knew you were lying. I always had a feeling you had another family," Chance says.

"I don't have another family. You are all going to find out how foolish you are and that I have done nothing."

The marriage disintegrated as Rae stood watching her husband pointlessly scramble to piece together what had fallen away. He searched for messages that did not exist, words that could not heal, and a woman who no longer felt for him. She just watched. Blankly staring. No words. When he realized that there was no means of reparations, he left. The air was no longer suffocating from the space he was filling.

She breathed. The pressure remained.

*T*his chapter deals with self-harm, betrayal, emotional abuse, and dissociation. If this reflection brings up difficult emotions, consider reaching out to someone safe or a professional support resource. You do not have to hold this alone.

**Reflective Activity: When Trust Quietly Shifts Chapter 4**

Purpose:

This activity invites reflection on how trust is built, how self-protection can soften into vulnerability, and how silence—our own or others'—can become dangerous. Readers are encouraged to notice emotional shifts, patterns of belief, and moments when truth is postponed in the name of survival.

Take your time. You may journal, voice-note, draw, or simply sit with the questions. Answer only what feels safe.

Part I: Noticing the Softening Rae begins this chapter guarded, disciplined, and intentional—yet slowly softens in Michael's presence. Reflective Prompts:

Think about a time when someone felt safe to you.

What made them feel safe—consistency, kindness, patience, familiarity?

Have you ever confused absence of harm with presence of care?

What parts of yourself tend to soften first when you begin trusting someone?

Journal Line:

"I begin to trust when."

________________________."

Part II: The Stories We Tell Ourselves

Rae accepts reassurances that allow her to stay aligned with what she wants to

believe, even when unease exists beneath the surface.

Reflective Prompts:

Have you ever held onto a belief because it helped you survive a season—even if it wasn't fully true?

What lies tend to sound the most convincing when you are tired, lonely, or overwhelmed?

Is there a difference between being deceived and choosing not to look too closely?

Journal Line:

"The lie I needed to believe at the time was

__________________________________."

Part III: Silence as Survival

Rae cuts. She endures. She carries truths alone. Silence becomes a coping mechanism.

Reflective Prompts:

What has silence protected you from? What has silence cost you?

Who noticed your pain—but didn't ask—and how did that feel?

Optional Reflection:

Write about something you survived by not speaking. No explanation needed—just acknowledgment.

Part IV: The Body Remembers

This chapter shows how betrayal and prolonged stress live in the body—

through self-harm, dissociation, pregnancy complications, collapse.

Body Awareness Check-In:

Pause. Breathe slowly.

Where do you feel tension right now?

Does your body feel heavy, numb, tight, or restless?

If your body could speak one sentence, what would it say?

 Journal Line:

"My body has been holding

_______________________________________."

Part V: When Truth Arrives Unprotected Rae learns devastating truth from a stranger —not the person who owed her honesty.

Reflective Prompts:

Have you ever received life-altering information in an unprotected way?

What did you need in that moment that you did not receive?

What would protected truth have looked like?

🖊 Letter Prompt (Optional):

Write a short note to yourself beginning with:

"You deserved to hear the truth with

_________________________."

Closing Grounding Practice

Place one hand on your chest and one on your abdomen.

Take three slow breaths.

Silently repeat:

I survived what I didn't deserve. I am allowed to breathe now.

## Chapter 5 Wise Counsel

Over the next few months, her mind slowly caved under the weight of betrayal, and the crushing

heartache it birthed. Finding herself back in a place where her health was declining and her body was betraying her, Rae was hospitalized. Recovery was frustrating and unending due to the doctor's initial inability to determine the source of the illness. Testing for a brain bleed, stroke, neurological disorders, and heart conditions were conducted and ruled out. It was difficult to comprehend how a healthy, young woman could struggle to walk or form coherent sentences. Inadvertently, she would lose her job. As the cabinets emptied, her sense of security thinned with them. Friends and family encouraged her to apply for food benefits through the state until she was able to secure employment and get back on her feet. The belief that she was taking resources meant for someone else pressed painfully against her sense of worth. Realizing that what she was carrying was heavier than what she was capable of handling, she sought treatment.

Reaching out to a trusted friend, was difficult. Admitting that she needed someone, something outside of herself was humbling. "Rae, I could work with you, but I have someone in mind who may be an even better fit. Her therapeutic approach is very similar to my own."

Releasing a sigh that reflected how hard it

was to admit she was not okay—only to be redirected—was not easy.

"Okay. May I have the contact information?"

"She's, my cousin. Her name is Danielle."

A calm swept over Rae, not from having an experience with this unknown individual but hearing she shared a similar style, and she was her family. Rae unexplainably felt safe.

The first session with Danielle was riddled with surprise and feelings Rae was not prepared to unleash. Believing she could keep things surface-level, she planned to avoid facing what was hurting her.

"Rayanne, tell me about your marriage."

"It's been built on a lie. All these years, I thought I gave my husband a family, I gave him a son only to learn some random female who meant nothing— found her way in our lives." Tears built up, and her words got stuck as they formed. She looked toward the openness beyond the clear glass square— rich, robust trees beneath calm blue skies. In that moment, her heart burst.

The words plaguing her rolled off her tongue.

"Women tend to believe we always looks at the other woman as the culprit."

"Well, is that the case?"

"No. I see both as horrifyingly disgusting, but I married my husband. All I asked for was honesty."

For weeks the person Rayanne's husband slept with was referred to as "that woman", "That whore," "her," but never her name.

"Rayanne, this will always hold power over you until you are ready to speak her name. Mya. I will not force you, but I encourage you to try it."

"I'm not ready."

"Before we close, is there anything you want to talk about?"

"No"

"Is next Monday's standing session okay."

"Yes."

"I will see you then."

The months ahead dragged Rayanne through an emotional and mental stretch she didn't know she could survive. In the midst of healing from her husband's betrayal, she received the diagnosis of breast cancer. Her therapist would be the first to learn of the diagnosis. She sat across from her on the firm navy-blue sofa, lined with thoughtfully chosen pillows. Something to be shared was fixed in the outline of her forced smile, and soulful eyes.

"Rae?"

"Danielle, I have cancer. I'm not upset. I'm not even scared. I really don't know how to feel."

"And that's ok."

"When I got the call, I knew. I just knew. I haven't told anyone."

"Why? Why are you choosing to walk this alone?"

"I don't have an answer for that."

"It always goes back to when will Rayanne be worthy enough to be considered. You don't have to answer that in this moment. But what would you like to talk about today?"

Rayanne was able to release part of what she

had been holding throughout the week. As she spoke, the tension moved through her body, settling in her legs—creating a restless pull that made sitting still feel nearly impossible. Her fingers twitched, her feet pressed into the floor, as if the memories were finding their way out through her extremities. Her physical state shifted—her muscles relaxed, and her breathing slowed.

"How are you feeling in your body? "Fine."

"Is there anything else you wish to talk about before we close?"

"No."

"Okay, If we're ok to meet, I will see you next Tuesday."

That evening, as the house grew quiet and the night closed in, Rae felt the familiar weight of struggle rise within her. Holding her Bible close, she searched for scripture about strength and restraint, hoping the words would steady her. Yet even as she read, a deep desire to numb the emotional pain lingered, pulling her attention away from the page. The verses blurred, overtaken by an insatiable urge to quiet the ache inside her chest.

Sanguine liquid glided down the sides of her arm. It was warm and intoxicating. The euphoria known in that moment, was suffocating. Sinking into its allure was both inviting and scary. What if she never came up for air? What if she allowed herself to sink so deeply that she crossed a point of no return? What if her actions ultimately led to her death? If this were a session with her therapist Danielle, she wouldn't bother parlaying in decorative language. She'd skip the fancy words and get straight to the point. In her forwardness, she'd say, "Do you want to die?" There were days when the answer to that question was an emphatic "YES." Then, there were days Rae just wanted to be free. She wanted live in freedom not carting the heaviness of her heart.

It dawned on her that she was in a fight for her life, and no one was rushing in—no one had been told there was a war happening within her. Why? She smiled, a soft and practiced smile. Then she responded with "I'm fine" when asked, "How are you?" The truth is she was unraveling. Her old friend who met her in the living room years ago, revisited her and stared her down. "You're not fine. Your heart is heavy, and I can help you."

Rae's sister once told her that her battle made her sister feel as if she was standing outside a locked door, hearing her screams but there was no handle. She could not gain access to her. "Let me in!" She exclaimed.

Rae made the conscious choice to fight alone for years due to shame, embarrassment and guilt. The gradual decline of her mental health was directly impacted to the stigma placed on having depression, anxiety or mood-altering diagnoses. How can a woman of faith declare that she believes while drowning in the undertow of life happenings? In her belief, you're not expected to handle it alone, yet she felt alone.

In the depths of night, when the house was hushed and her thoughts thundered, there you were. Impulsivity tore through every thought, leaving her unguarded. The intensity grew, as Rayanne held her breath holding back cries and screams. Clawing at the backside of her hand, as her skin lifts.

Stubborn in its hold, refusing to relinquish its power, she clawed deeper but on the underside of her wrist. Breaking the skin, watching as trails of blood circled her arm, dripping onto her lap. Relief no longer felt impervious but tangible-within reach. The deeper she clawed, the more each slit whispered a dark relief. Rayanne pushed further into the ache, convincing herself that each break in the tension was relief.

Each moment she endured became proof that relief does not come from harm, but from resilience. Even in the darkest hours, she found that she could survive the storm.

One evening, Rayanne prepared for the night believing silence would hold no calls, no interruptions, no one would find her in the quiet. Then. . . Kisha called, shifting the trajectory of her night. She needed a steady voice to stay with her as she drove home. Holding her razor in hand along with swabs and gauze, Rayanne paused.

Packaging each back into her bag and speaking as if the actions taking place, were normal activities.

Standing before the mirror, she studied her reflection and the scars her illness had left behind. She remembered a time when the shadows felt like safety, when the lies she etched into her own mind became easier to believe. Her gaze dropped to the empty pill bottle in her hand—no refills left—and she smiled faintly. There was a time when discouragement ransacked her thoughts, leaving her convinced her mind would never be whole again. Desperate to prove she didn't need medication, Rayanne would abruptly stop taking it, only to spiral back into a part of her mind filled with fear and an ugliness she had worked hard to keep sealed away.

 Rayanne had slipped into a deep depression one that allowed her to function but not to feel present. The world moved forward while she remained still. Each day, she showed up to her post wearing her many titles, reliable, present, capable, yet feeling profoundly disconnected beneath them. Her body moved through routine, but her mind lagged, heavy with thoughts she could not quiet. Even in moments of stillness, there was no rest. The exhaustion wasn't loud; it settled in quietly, lingering in her chest and behind her eyes, making presence feel like performance rather than living.

Showing up for work became both a necessary distraction, a place to breathe and a temporary pause from the tension building at home—the guilt that whispered she was failing as a mother, and from being pulled back into a version of herself she thought she had moved beyond.

A notification from her psychologist requesting a virtual visit in 15 minutes. Rayanne was not obligated to be in meetings or with students and set that time aside. "Hi Rayanne, its Dr. Houston. How are you feeling today?"

"Hi Dr. Houston. I hope all has been well on your end. I have been feeling very sad. This sadness is dark and heavy and scares me. I don't like the weight of it, and I don't know how to manage it. I do take accountability for my part in my spiraling.

I stopped taking my medication when I noticed that my sadness was turning into depression. I knew that wasn't my doing. But when I stopped the medication, it hurled me into a deep depression, and the cutting went from seldom to daily. Then I started cutting multiple times a day."

"Ray, I'm glad you shared this. What you're describing sounds scary and heavy, and it makes sense that it would feel overwhelming—especially with the medication change layered on top of everything else. I hear how much weight you're carrying, and how honest you're being about your part in it. That kind of clarity takes courage.

I do want to pause and check in with you gently: are you safe right now? If the urges to hurt yourself feel strong or hard to manage, you deserve immediate support—not alone time with that pain."

"I feel safe. I have a good support system both at work and home."

"Rayanne, a few important things to name, without judgment:

stopping medication abruptly can seriously intensify depression and distress. That isn't a failure, it's a physiological response.

The increase in self-harm isn't a moral issue;

it's a sign your system is overwhelmed and needs support. This level of sadness is not something you're meant to manage by yourself.

I plan to reach out to both the Oncologist and Psychiatrist

prescribing and managing your medication as soon as possible and tell them exactly what's been happening."

"Ok."


"I want you to know that if you're struggling more than usual you can call or text 988 (Suicide & Crisis Lifeline) any time—day or night. It's free and confidential. You don't have to hold this alone. I'm here with you. Help is available. You'll reach someone who is trained to listen and support you.

"Ok."

"This information does concern me, Rayanne. An acute facility may be the next option but I will speak with the team and follow up with you."

"Ok."

"Do you have any questions for me?"

"No," Rayanne had the urge to run and fast but smiled through an uncomfortable setting.

 "Rayanne, I know this is not easy for you. I will be speaking with you very soon."

The mention of an acute facility fractured Rayanne's focus. Her thoughts scattered, then rushed, seeking somewhere, anywhere, to land outside her mind. The sensation moved through her limbs in restless surges until it became unbearable. She retreated inward, reaching for familiar but destructive ways to silence the noise.

The relief came fast and faded just as quickly. Rayanne hid away and pulled from her satchel a razor, alcohol pad and gauze. Each slit created release from the pressure building within.

"God, I don't want this for my life anymore! I keep saying that I desire to be free. I was asked, 'what am I willing to do differently to be free?'" It is time I take up my bed and walk (ref John 5:8) Healing is my portion!

*This chapter contains themes of self-harm, depression, medical trauma, and suicidal ideation. If these reflections bring up intense emotions, please reach out to a trusted person or professional support. In the U.S., you can call or text 988 for immediate, confidential support.*

*You are worthy of care before, during, and after healing.*

**Reflective Activity: When Strength Means Reaching Out Chapter 5**

Purpose:

This chapter explores the quiet bravery of asking for help, the danger of isolation disguised as independence, and the healing power of wise counsel—both human and divine. This reflection invites readers to examine where they have struggled alone, how stigma has shaped their silence, and what it might mean to choose support without shame.

You are not required to answer everything. Pause where your body tells you to. Care for yourself as you reflect.

Part I: When the Body Speaks What the Mouth Cannot

Rae's body collapses under what her spirit has been carrying—before her mind is ready to name it.

Reflective Prompts:

Has your body ever signaled distress before you consciously admitted something was wrong?

What symptoms (fatigue, numbness, illness, restlessness) have you ignored or minimized in yourself?

How do you usually respond when your body says, "This is too much"?

 Journal Line:

"My body has been trying to tell me

__________________________________."

Part II: The Weight of Worthiness

Rae struggles with accepting help—financial, emotional, medical—because of a belief that needing support diminishes her value.

Reflective Prompts:

Where did you learn that needing help equals weakness?

Have you ever felt undeserving of care because "someone else needs it more"?

What would it mean to believe that your need is not a moral failure?

 Journal Line:

"When I need help, the story I tell myself is

__________________________________."

Part III: Wise Counsel vs. Familiar Silence

Rae seeks help—but even then, tries to stay surface-level, hoping to avoid what hurts most.

Reflective Prompts:

When you open, what topics feel off-limits, even in safe spaces?

Who in your life has earned the right to hear your truth—but you've kept outside the door?

What fears surface when someone asks the right question?

✎ Name It Gently:

Is there a truth you've delayed naming because it feels too powerful.

Part IV: Naming What Holds Power

Rae's therapist challenges her to speak the

name she avoids—because unnamed pain often controls us.

Reflective Prompts:

Is there a word, name, diagnosis, memory, or truth you resist saying out loud?

What do you fear will happen if you name it?

What power might lessen if you did?

Optional Exercise:

Write the thing you've avoided naming. You do not need to explain it. Simply acknowledge it exists.

Part V: Faith, Shame, and the Myth of Doing It Alone

Rae wrestles with the belief that faith should make suffering quieter, cleaner, or easier.

**Reflective Prompts:**

114

Have you ever felt that your faith disqualified your pain?

Were you taught—explicitly or implicitly—that believers shouldn't struggle this way?

How has shame distorted your understanding of spiritual strength?

 Reframe:

"My faith does not require my silence. It invites

_______________________________."

Part VI: When Coping Turns Costly

This chapter does not romanticize self-harm—it reveals it as a survival strategy that eventually demands intervention.

Reflective Prompts (Answer only what feels safe):

What coping strategies once protected you but now harm you?

What need were they trying to meet?

If relief didn't require pain, what might you reach for instead?

🖊 Compassion Statement:

"I was trying to survive when I

______________________________. That matters."

## Part VII: Letting Someone Stay With You

Kisha's call interrupts a dangerous moment —not with answers, but with presence.

Reflective Prompts:

Who has ever stayed with you in the middle of your storm—physically or emotionally?

Who could you allow to stay with you now?

What keeps you from letting people know when it's critical?

Circle of Care:

List one person you could contact when the weight feels unbearable.


Closing Grounding Reflection Place your feet on the floor.

Take a slow breath in through your nose, and out through your mouth.

Silently affirm:

I am not required to heal in isolation. Wise counsel is not weakness—it is wisdom.

# Chapter 6 She Healed

I would love to say that one morning Rayanne awakened, and the urges had completely disappeared. That light spilled effortlessly through her window each day, even when the skies were gray and heavy with rain. But that was not her story. What is true is this: help had been there all along. Hands outstretched, steady, patiently waiting while she struggled in the undertow. Rayanne did not rise because the water calmed. She rose because she finally chose not to fight alone. This time, Rae reached back. She extended her hand and accepted what was offered without shame or apology and accepted help. That became the turning point.

As she stepped into her healing, she turned from the mirror taking one last glance and truly saw herself. She was no longer focused on those things external of her. She saw Rayanne. The urge to hide and cope through self-inflicted pain was no longer there. The pills she relied on to steady her emotions and body were gone, the last refill now empty. It wasn't the cutting that made her feel safe with her. It wasn't the dosing that made her feel safe with her.

"I feel safe with you!" She said staring at the healed version in the mirror.

# Epilogue

If you have made it to this page, pause for a moment. Let that matter. You did not arrive here by accident. You arrived here because you stayed through the uncomfortable parts, the heavy moments, the questions that did not have neat answers. That takes courage. That takes honesty. That takes strength you may not always recognize in yourself. Whatever you are carrying, healing, grief, hope, exhaustion, or all of it at once you are not failing.

You are becoming. And becoming is brave work.

You are allowed to take breaks. You are allowed to ask for help. You are allowed to grow slowly, unevenly, and out loud.

Progress does not have to be loud to be real. Please

remember this:

You are not behind. You are not too much.

You are not alone in this.

You are capable. You are worthy of care. And you already have what it takes to keep going—one step, one breath, one honest moment at a time.

You are amazing. And you've got this!

# Notes

📞National Eating Disorders Helpline Alliance for Eating Disorders Awareness Call or Text: 1-800-931-2237

Live Chat: Available at https://www.allianceforeatingdisorders.com

Open daily with trained volunteers and clinicians

Offers support, referrals, and guidance for people struggling with eating disorders and for loved ones

🌐NEDA (National Eating Disorders Association)

Helpline: 1-800-931-2237

Text: NEDA to 741741 (crisis support)

Chat&resources:https://www.nationaleatingdisorders.org Provides education, support, recovery resources, and connections to treatment


988 Suicide & Crisis Lifeline Call or Text: 988

24/7, free, confidential support

Trained listeners can help you manage thoughts, crisis feelings, safety planning, and next steps

Crisis Text Line

Text: HOME to 741741

Available 24/7, private text support

RAINN (Rape, Abuse & Incest National Network)

Call: 1-800-656-HOPE (4673)

Online Chat: Available at https://ohl.rainn.org (click "Chat Now")

24/7, free & confidential support

Trained advocates can help you process what happened, talk through next steps, and connect you with local services.

🤍 You Don't Have to Go Through This Alone

These resources exist to support you without judgment, with confidentiality and respect.

# The Author

MaRisha Harris is an emerging author and breast cancer survivor whose journey began in May 2025 and continues to inspire her creative work. Through storytelling and artistic expression, she transforms lived experiences into meaningful literary pieces that center healing, emotion, and connection. MaRisha is the proud mother of four amazing children, who inspire her daily and stand as her greatest source of strength. She is equally proud of them and the growth they share together as a family.

Currently, MaRisha is pursuing her Licensed Professional Mental Health Counselor (LPMHC) credential, further deepening her commitment to social-emotional learning, advocacy, and supporting the emotional well-being of children and families.